RUMPUS

Planning behaviour groups for parents and carers of young children

by
Dr Hannah Mortimer
and
Catterick Garrison Health Visitors

A QEd Publication

Published in 2005

© Hannah Mortimer

ISBN 1 898873 43 7

British Library Cataloguing
A catalogue record for this book is available from the British Library.

Q⁄
Ed

Published by QEd Publications, Trent Park, Eastern Avenue,
Lichfield, Staffs. WS13 6RR
Web site: www.qed.uk.com
Email: orders@qed.uk.com

Printed in the United Kingdom by Stowes (Stoke-on-Trent).

Contents

Introduction

The aim of the series

This series is for those working in Sure Start centres and other early years practitioners who run parent and carer groups. In recent years, there has been a blossoming of Sure Start schemes all over the country with massive recruitment and intensive staff training as more and more schemes come on line. These books have been put together by practitioners who already have parent and carer groups up and running. They are the result of trying out approaches and evaluating their success and the hope is that they will provide practical ideas for colleagues starting new groups to prevent them having to reinvent the wheel. Inevitably, you will each be serving very individual communities with particular sets of needs, but it is hoped that you will find plenty of ideas in this series that will get you started.

Since the daily work of many Sure Start schemes is centred around family support and since this so often occurs in groups or 'drop-ins' held at a Sure Start base or community centre, these books are about how you make that delicate move from the informal 'drop in' to the kind of structure that will enable you to improve confidences, relationships and quality of communications between parents or carers and their children under five. The series includes books on:

RUMPUS Groups	behaviour management groups for parents or carers and their young children.
Step by Step Groups	groups that provide ideas and support to parents or carers to enable them to encourage their child's development (if the child is vulnerable or might have special needs).
Music and Play Groups	groups that provide circle time and structured play activities that improve relationships between parents or carers and their children.

Baby and Me   parent support groups that promote early
                        development, relationships and
                        communication in their babies.

Making Connections therapeutic groups for parents or carers to help
                        them form stronger attachments with their
                        children.

Sure Start

In Sure Start schemes, families are targeted to receive information, support and guidance to help them make the most of their young child's developmental, learning and social potential, and also to improve upon their parenting and child-rearing skills. The aim is to improve the life chances of young children in areas of 'risk', through improving their access to education, health services, family support and advice on nurturing. Typical Sure Start schemes provide a range of services and provision – there might be outreach and home visiting, support to families, support for good quality play, quality learning and childcare experiences for young children, advice on child and family health and support for families who have a young child with special educational needs (SEN) or other disability.

What is a RUMPUS group?

RUMPUS stands for 'Are you Mas and Pas under stress?' and is a user-friendly title for what is effectively a pre-school behaviour group. The title was developed by the Catterick Garrison Health Visiting team who are happy for others to use it so long as the source is acknowledged in any formal reports. These groups were developed by an educational and child psychologist, Hannah Mortimer, and a team of community health visitors in Catterick Garrison who hold regular RUMPUS groups in local health centres. The groups aim to support young parents and their early years children where there are particular difficulties in managing behaviour. A combination of approaches has been developed by the team to put parents at their ease, improve the attention skills of the children, encourage early language and interactive play, build up family relationships and provide

6

practical advice based on realistic expectations and week-by-week management of behaviour. Parents also make their own plans for encouraging positive behaviour in their children in a supportive atmosphere that aims to enable and empower rather than to prescribe. In this book, you will read about all these approaches and the model is now used as part of the menu of provision in the Stockton-on-Tees Borough Council Sure Start schemes.

What actually happens?

Each group has up to six families who come for six sessions, sometimes with one parent and sometimes with two. Often, there are several siblings under five who come too. Each set of parents or carers is worried about their child's behaviour or is feeling very stressed by family life. Each has asked for help and advice to manage the situation and has a home visit before the group starts to talk about what they need from it. Parents are told that they need to come to all six sessions to get the benefit. The groups are held in a large playroom and begin with a half-hour music and action rhyme session. This is to make it fun for the children and to help them to look, listen and join in. These are important skills when learning to behave and get on with others. It also helps the parents to see their children in the best light and to feel proud of them. Parents are encouraged not to worry if their child feels shy and wants to sit close to them and watch. After the music session there are drinks organised and a big box of toys is brought out for the children to play with. Some of the Sure Start team or crèche workers then play with the children, helping them to share, to settle any disputes and to get on together. They invite parents and carers to watch and they pass on ideas if these are asked for.

Where does the behaviour management come in?

While this is going on, the parents talk with a psychologist, health visitor or other specialist about their child's behaviour. They are sometimes asked to keep a diary sheet that will help them plan how to change the situation and they are supported by the team through the first few weeks as they put their plan into practice. The parents and carers usually find each other a good source of support and good use is made of encouraging families to work in pairs or groups of three. At the sixth session, parents and carers are asked to fill in an evaluation form. By then, some families will feel they are now managing better though others will wish to continue to talk with their health visitor or a Sure Start worker or even be referred to a more specialist service such as a CAMHS Team (Child and Adolescent Mental Health Service).

What parents and carers say

'She started to settle with coming to the group. And she loved the music.'

'I just needed ideas on what to do about the tantrums. They still happen, but I know how I want to tackle them now.'

It was a relief to meet .... who was having the same difficulties.'

'As a dad, I felt it was good to be part of it. I've never seen her play with other children before.'

'I couldn't believe he played so well in the group.'

How to use this book

You now have an overview of what a RUMPUS group might look like.

- In Chapter 1, you are prompted to consider when and why you might like to run such a group, when to do it, how it might fit into the Sure Start framework of provision or indeed into the early years service that you offer.

- Chapter 2 helps you plan ahead – what you need in terms of equipment, personnel, premises and skills.

- In Chapter 3 there are suggestions for arranging a home visit and setting up the sessions, together with a questionnaire you can use to gauge stress levels and invite parents to state what they would like to see changed in their child's behaviour.

- Chapter 4 gives you many suggestions for the music session at the beginning of the group and is accessible at any level of musical ability – you do not need to be musical yourself.

- In Chapter 5 there are suggestions for crèche workers who will be entertaining the children.

- Chapter 6 covers the behaviour management structure that lends itself to this kind of group, complete with record sheet and celebration certificate.

- Chapter 7 contains suggestions for evaluation and reporting back to management committees. There are some helpful resources and contacts listed at the back of the book.

Throughout the book there are ideas and suggestions from practitioners who have actually developed and run these groups. These should help you to understand why certain approaches were used and what the particular challenges and opportunities were in running the groups.

Chapter 1

Why have a RUMPUS group?

In this chapter, you are prompted to consider when and why you might like to run such a group and how it might fit into the Sure Start framework of provision, or indeed into the more general early years service that you offer.

We knew that Sure Start schemes should start with the families – what they needed rather than what we felt they needed – but how could we be sure we were targeting the people that needed our support most? We could see that certain parents were not attached to their children and that they were not getting the pleasure from each other that they should – but how do you get that across to a family? We can hardly tell them 'You've got an attachment problem!' So we had to approach the whole thing more indirectly. That's where RUMPUS came in.

(Sure Start practitioner)

RUMPUS in primary healthcare

It was in the primary healthcare situation that we first developed RUMPUS groups, based in local health centres. Perhaps you work as a team of health visitors, community therapists, nursery nurses or voluntary workers and are thinking of starting a group for parents and carers who are having difficulties in managing the behaviour of their pre-school children.

In the past, professionals would tend to bring parents and carers together and plan a series of sessions, each with a focus on a particular kind of behaviour and often with a visiting 'expert' to talk about feeding difficulties, sleeping difficulties or temper tantrums. This is certainly one way of approaching things, but it tended to give the message that '*we* are the experts, not the parents' and was also based very much on what *professionals* saw was needed rather than what parents and carers were asking for.

Those of us who worked in this kind of model often found that attendance fell rapidly as soon as it was recognised that we had no magic wands to wave. We also found that those families who were most stressed lacked the confidence, the energy or the opportunity to attend regularly. They certainly would not entrust their particular problems to unfamiliar professionals with plenty of stock answers. We would find fairly early on in the group that the best attenders were those families who were interested and motivated in their parenting but that we 'lost' those who needed the support most. It was this kind of thinking that led to the formation of RUMPUS groups in primary health settings such as local health clinics.

Looking back, we were probably weeding out the parents and carers who were connected and motivated by their parenting from those who were not, for whatever reason. Now that we know more about patterns of attachment between parents and their children, we can begin to identify those who are successfully 'connected' or 'bonded' from those who are not. One health visitor, Karen Bibbings, has devised this simple activity to explain what 'connection' looks like.

The Glums

Below is a scenario that could be used as a staff discussion point.

Imagine you are sitting in a restaurant. In one corner, there is a couple who are obviously deeply in love. We will call them 'the lovers'. How do you know that they are in love? What behaviours do you actually observe? Make a list of these on a large sheet of paper.

Now imagine you are in the same restaurant and in another corner is a couple who are clearly not getting on very well. We will call them 'the Glums'. What do you actually see or hear this time? Make another list.

Things to consider:
• Think about carers and children who are 'attached' or 'connected' to each other. Do you observe similar behaviours as 'the lovers' and 'the Glums'?

- You now know what a connected child and carer look like. Can you also recognise when such a connection is not there?

- Think of ways you can support attachments/connections by helping carers 'tune in' to their children and to share pleasure in each other.

From an activity by Karen Bibbings, Health Visitor, Stockton-on-Tees Sure Start (with permission)

Patterns of attachment

There are some children whose challenging behaviour is very resistant to change. These are the children who can settle better if given 'secure attachment figures' to relate to who can support, offer consistency of handling, and be there to reassure and to encourage. Attachment Theory argues that children develop a style of relating to important attachment figures in their lives, which secures for them the best parenting available under the circumstances.

The study of attachments has opened up a whole new way of assessing family relationships and providing therapeutic support. The patterns of attachment remain remarkably consistent over time until the child is about six and so can be observed, identified and worked with. Many of these parents find that their pre-school children are difficult to control, extremely angry and aggressive, or highly anxious and 'clingy'. Therapists might have tried to teach them behavioural management techniques, but where there is an attachment difficulty, the behaviour tends to persist, partly because the emotional climate and the relationships are not conducive to change.

Where attachment is working securely, an infant's cries and demands will be met reliably with sensitivity and warmth by the carer and the growing child develops in confidence and independence. We know this because of the influential research of John Bowlby and colleagues into bonding, attachment and loss. If a parent is unresponsive or rejects their cries of distress, that child may act as if they are independent long before they are emotionally ready to be. They may pay little attention when their parent leaves them at nursery and seldom look at their parent or try to involve them in their play. This is known as a pattern of 'anxious-avoidant' attachment.

If a parent is inconsistent in their responses, perhaps because of periods of depression, or frequent absences, the child learns to cry or shout louder with their demands, producing a pattern of 'ambivalent' attachment. There is also a pattern of 'disorganised' or 'controlling' attachment in which children develop a very controlling style over their parent in order to maintain some degree of predictability or structure in their lives. This pattern is common with parents who might have suffered loss, trauma or abuse themselves, or lack a 'secure base' of their own from which to provide nurture and care to others in their lives. Understanding about attachments does not mean that we should go forth and proclaim that a parent or child 'has an attachment disorder'. However, it does help us to understand that there is an emotional component to the behaviour or the relationship which may involve us trying to intervene on an emotional level as well as a behavioural or teaching level.

Which families benefit most from RUMPUS?

In the author's experience, diagnosing attachment disorder is not always 'black and white' – indeed, there are many 'shades of grey'. Using the example of 'the Glums', it becomes possible to identify that a parent or carer and a child are having *difficulties* in connecting and that effective intervention at the level of primary healthcare can and does promote positive change. These are the families who would benefit from RUMPUS. If there is a more serious and entrenched attachment disorder, then more specialist provision would be needed. We have often tried a RUMPUS intervention first, and then decided to explore a referral to the local CAMHS Team if it does not prove effective.

To sum up, RUMPUS groups are most effective for families:

- of children under five where parenting is stressful and behaviour difficult to manage;

- where the parent and carer has mild to moderate difficulties in connecting to one or more of the young children;

- who have been working with their health visitor or other professional to change their young child's difficult behaviour but where something more seems to be needed.

We have not found RUMPUS helpful for:

- parents or carers who have their own mental health problems;

- families with severe attachment disorders (though the group can help us identify those who need more specialist support);

- families who, for whatever reason, cannot attend regularly.

We have found RUMPUS to be just as effective for children with all levels of ability, regardless of disability or special need. In that respect, this is an inclusive provision. We also found that it fitted most easily where there was a whole scaffold of support – for example, antenatal care groups, post-natal support groups, 'Roller-coaster groups' (for post-natal depression), 'Little Monkeys' (for the usual range of toddler behaviours) and 'Hugs and Tugs' (for more entrenched attachment difficulties).

RUMPUS in Sure Start

It seemed a small step to take the RUMPUS model and develop it to fit the Sure Start framework. It was developed in Stockton-on-Tees Sure Start Services where there are many schemes serving urban and diverse communities. We again saw it as fitting into a wider framework of provision in which parents and carers fell into three main categories:

- Hard-to-reach – they need support but may not ask for it or even want it.

- Mainstream – they both need and want support.

- Easy-to-reach – they probably do not really need support but want it anyway.

We decided that within the Sure Start philosophy, provision should be offered inclusively to all these categories and that it should be available at three stages of family life:

- 'Bump Club' – prenatal support.

- 'New Arrivals' – early days of parenting.

- 'Parent/carer and toddler' – the pre-school years.

This kind of thinking enables one to draw up a grid of support, making sure that each category of parent has access to support at different family life stages. For the hard-to-reach families, you might opt for a home visiting model as a first stage towards involving that family in more group-based activity and support. We saw RUMPUS as fitting into the framework for supporting 'mainstream' families at the 'parent/carer and toddler' stage. In other words, RUMPUS is helpful for parents and carers who both want and need support in managing the behaviour of their pre-school children. The optimum number of families per RUMPUS group is five or six and never more than eight or less than four. You need enough to encourage sharing and mutual support, but not so many that you cannot make sure everyone is supported and happy.

Chapter 2

Planning ahead

In this chapter, information is provided to help you plan ahead – what you need in terms of equipment, personnel, premises and skills. Suppose you have a cohort of five or six families that you would like to plan a RUMPUS group for. This is what you need to do next.

Finding a room

We have found that the best space to use is a large, carpeted room with the opportunity for seating one end and play the other. In this kind of 'mainstream' group, we found that the advantages of having parents and children in the same room far outweighed the distractions that this caused. This:

- allowed those of us working with the parents or carers to observe the children as we talked together;·

- allowed the children to come and go freely if they needed extra attention or reassurance from their parents;

- allowed those of us playing with the children to 'model' appropriate ways of interacting with them;

- allowed parents and carers to feel proud of their children's behaviour in the group;

- avoided the feeling that we were taking their children away to 'therap' them because we were the experts.

At all times, we respected the parents' and carers' role in parenting and dealing with their own children, though we also displayed a clear 'No Smacking Zone' sign on the entrance.

Just occasionally, we found it helpful to have a separate room to withdraw to with a professional. For example, we used this when one parent was particularly tearful or when we were working with twins who were continually upsetting each other. You also need access to a kitchen area and to family-friendly toilets and wash areas. We have run RUMPUS groups effectively in health centres, Sure Start bases, community centres, school rooms and church halls.

Staffing

For the usual number of six families, you need these people to work with parents or carers:

- two or three professionals who are used to working with and supporting families where there are behaviour issues (a ratio of one professional to two families). These might include health visitors, Sure Start workers, community nurses, positive parenting trainers, primary mental health workers, Portage workers, early years teachers or trainee psychologists;

- one clinical/educational psychologist.

You also need adults to play with the children. Depending on the numbers and ages of children and siblings and their particular needs, you need one adult to every one to three children. These could be Sure Start play facilitators, play volunteers (who have had the usual police checks), crèche workers, trainee nurses or nursery nurses, and any visiting health visitors or other child-care professionals. In addition, you need one adult to be in charge of the play session and set any structured activities. This person would normally have a nursery nurse or early years education qualification.

Booking play equipment

Arrange for a selection of attractive and safe toys and playthings suitable for the range of ages and interests you are catering for. The local toy library might be able to help you if you do not have these already available (see details of the National Association of Toy and Leisure Libraries on page 53). Be aware that children under three might swallow small items. We use a core of pop-up toys and activity centres, giant floor puzzles, cars and road layouts, dolls and prams and large-scale construction toys – and then we vary it a little week by week. In addition, you might find it helpful to plan one structured activity such as hand painting, play dough or collage each session. Finally, you need a box of musical instruments (see Chapter 4) and a notebook for each family.

Transport

Look for a base that is easy to get to using public transport and which has safe and convenient parking for family cars and buggies. You might also be able to make use of local hospital transport services or Sure Start transport vehicles. If the cost of transport is going to be prohibitive for some families, consider building in a travel allowance for families into the budget.

Refreshments ·

There is an element of nurturing within the RUMPUS group and, to do this, you need a convenient kitchen nearby with facilities for making parents and carers drinks and providing juice and refreshments for the children. We tend to use healthy snacks with a selection of fruit pieces and cheese. Make a point of asking parents what their child is allowed when handing out drinks and edibles. Be aware that the premises or service might have its own safety rules about hot drinks close to children playing. You might cover the cost of refreshments using a voluntary donation of a suggested amount. We felt that this helped parents and carers feel that they were able to contribute something themselves and we then subsidised any shortfall. Since many of the children would arrive already delving into a crisp packet or sucking a bottle, we would gradually use distraction and gentle suggestion to reduce this 'feeding by grazing' behaviour and move on to healthy and sociable snack-times.

Inviting the families

You need to think about what information you are going to give the families ahead of the group sessions. Consider whether you will be selecting the families and approaching them to see if they would like to come or allowing for self-selection. We tend to use self-selection in Sure Start and invitations in primary health settings. We also found that RUMPUS developed best if it arose naturally out of other groups and out of expressed wishes from parents: 'Where can I talk about her behaviour more?' 'How can I get more help?' Therefore, we tended to start with a simple drop-in group for coffee and play, moving onto a RUMPUS group for certain of the families who wanted it. Another book in this series, *Music and Play*, covers what these drop-in groups might look like.

Here is an example of the kind of information sheet you might use (with acknowledgement to both the Catterick Garrison and Stockton-on-Tees Sure Start RUMPUS teams). If you wish, you can photocopy it back-to-back to make a folded A5-size pamphlet (enlarge it to A4 first, then fold it to A5). Where necessary or desirable, you should take the trouble of producing the pamphlet in different languages.

RUMPUS

R You Mas and Pas Under Stress?

Where is the group held?

When?

Timing for the groups will be .... on the following dates:

. . . . .

What happens if my child is ill or if I can't come?

Please let us know in advance if you are not able to come to a session on Tel: ....

Welcome!

We hope you find the sessions useful. Please let us know if you have any ideas for improving them ... we are here to listen.

What is a RUMPUS group?

Each group has up to six families who come for six sessions. Each one of you is worried about your child's behaviour and has asked for help and advice to manage it. You need to come to all six sessions to get the benefit.

Who will we meet?

Before the group starts, someone from Sure Start will visit you at home to tell you more about it. The group is held in a large playroom. You will meet the other families and Sure Start workers.

You will also meet one or more of the health visitors and a child psychologist.

What will happen?

First of all, there is a half-hour music session. This is to make it fun for the children and to help them to look, listen and join in. These are important skills when learning to behave and get on with others. Don't worry if your child feels shy and wants to sit close to you and watch. We will sing songs, play listening games and then join in with musical instruments to a tape.

After the music, we will entertain the children in the same room, giving you a chance to talk about your child's behaviour.

What help do we get with behaviour?

After the music session there will be drinks and a big box of toys is brought out for the children to play with. Some of the Sure Start team will be playing with your children, helping them to share, settle any disputes and to get on together. They invite you to watch and pass on ideas to you.

You may be asked to keep a diary sheet that will help you plan how to change the situation and support you through the first few weeks. You will usually find the other parents a good support; they know what you are going through.

What happens at the end of the sessions?

At the sixth session you will be asked to fill in an evaluation form. Some families will feel they are now managing; some will continue to talk with their health visitor or a Sure Start worker or be referred on to a more specialist service.

What parents say

'She started to settle with coming to the group. And she loved the music.'

'I just needed ideas on what to do about the tantrums. They still happen but I know how I want to tackle them now.'

'It was a relief to meet .... who was having the same difficulties.'

'As a dad, I felt it was good to be part of it. I've never seen her play with other children before.'

'I couldn't believe he played so well in the group.'

Chapter 3

Introducing the families

In this chapter, there are suggestions for arranging home visits and planning the sessions, together with a questionnaire you can use to gauge stress levels and invite parents to state what they would like to see changed in their child's behaviour. In the first chapter we introduced the kind of families that RUMPUS might be most effective for. This is what to do next.

The RUMPUS planning meeting

This is a meeting of about an hour-and-a-half with the key professionals involved to:

• discuss which families to invite;

• introduce their needs to each other;

• set up home visits;

• agree six dates (we have found a regular weekly slot to be the best);

• make sure there are enough staff to cover the families and children;

• check that premises and equipment are available;

• plan the time of the evaluation meeting.

The initial home visit

We have found that the best way to introduce families to the group is by a home visit. It is a daunting process coming to a group and it makes all the difference in the world if the family can first meet with a friendly face in their own home and discuss what will be involved. The visit might be made by a professional who already knows the family (such as the health visitor or Sure Start worker involved) and it is helpful if this person is also involved with, or at least familiar with, what goes on in the RUMPUS group itself.

The purpose is to share with the family what the group is for and what will happen (the pamphlet on pages 20-21 should help with this). It is also an ideal time for finding out what the particular stresses and strains of the family are and what they would like to work on. The behaviour questionnaire below might be helpful to use or adapt as you require. Occasionally we have tried a more formalised assessment of parental stress such as the Parenting Stress Index – Short Form (Abidin, 1995) although we found this rather detailed for the 'mainstream' families we are working with. The home visit also allows you to find out who will be coming to the group (one parent or two and how many pre-school siblings and their ages – this allows you to plan staffing).

Behaviour questionnaire

Child's name: _____ Date of birth: _____

Parent's name/s: _____

What behaviours does your child have that are difficult to manage?
(Tick all that apply)

		Additional comments
Hits		
Kicks		
Bites		
Pulls hair		
Throws things		
Breaks things		
Abusive language		
Swears		
Head bangs		
Destructive		

		Additional comments
Doesn't do as I ask		
Temper tantrums		
Very clingy		
Other (please tell us what)		
What have you tried so far?		
Sending to his/her room		
Time out (e.g. to stairs)		
Arguing		
Saying 'No'		
Explaining		
Ignoring		
Getting angry		
Punishing (please say how)		
Praising good behaviour		
Giving in		
What would you like changed?		
What behaviour do you want to see *less* of?		
What behaviour do you want to see *more* of?		

The group timetable

When planning your group, make sure that you allow time for the professionals to meet and plan before and after each session. We have found that this needs to be made a clear priority because otherwise professionals tend to skip or foreshorten these times and the effectiveness of the group becomes diluted and loses its direction. This is a timetable that we have used in different settings that you can adapt to suit your own situation.

Timetable	
9.00–9.30a.m.	Meet to plan session, agree goals and set out equipment.
9.30a.m.	Parents arrive.
9.40–10.00a.m.	Music time.
10.00a.m.	Refreshments and play.
10.10–10.55a.m.	Adults' session as the children play.
10.55a.m.	Tidy up time and goodbye song. Families leave.
11.00–11.30a.m.	Professionals review the session and share goals for the next.

When planning your times, make sure that they fit in with local drop-off and collection times for any siblings at nursery and school. It is also worth adding at this point that some evaluations have suggested that six sessions are not enough and that eight to ten would be better. You will need to decide what suits your families and your context best. We did find that it was essential to arrange the sessions at weekly intervals and at the same time each week. Whenever we tried to change this (usually to suit professionals rather than families), we 'lost' a family or two in the process. Never assume that everyone regulates their lives by diaries in the same way that professionals do.

The follow-up home visit

In between the last session and the RUMPUS evaluation meeting, home visits should be made (usually by the same person who did the initial home visit) in order to talk through how the group went and discuss whether further support is needed. At this point, an evaluation questionnaire can be used (see the example in Chapter 7 on page 48).

The RUMPUS evaluation meeting

This usually takes place about three weeks after the last RUMPUS session. It is a one-and-a-half hour meeting with the key professionals to:

- review the follow-up home visits;

- arrange any necessary follow-up/referral for the families;

- agree who writes up the evaluation report and to whom it should be sent;

- discuss any revisions to procedure, premises, equipment, timetables;

- set date for next RUMPUS planning meeting.

Chapter 4

Music making

In this chapter there are many suggestions for the music session at the beginning of the group. This session is accessible to all . . . regardless of musical ability. This also applies to whoever leads the session – you do not need to be musical.

Why music?

Over the years the author has found that professionals are horrified at the suggestion that they should start the RUMPUS session with a music time – 'We're not musical!' 'The families will be embarrassed!' 'The children won't sit still.' Time and time again, groups have been persuaded to 'have a go' and time and time again, they have reported back that the music makes *all the difference.*

Music is an amazing thing – it stills a crying baby; it captures a toddler's attention; it holds the interest of children who, in any other situation, might be experiencing considerable behaviour or communication difficulties. It provides opportunities for even very young children to join together sociably in a group, long before they are old enough to attend an early years setting. Music encourages children who do not like to look and to listen to do just that. It provides a 'level playing field' for professionals and families to break the ice together – after all, neither is the 'expert' and both will find themselves sharing a laugh or a grimace as the process rarely goes as expected! But most importantly, the children are *captivated* and sometimes, for the first time ever, parents and carers are seeing them look, listen and concentrate in a way they have never done before. This gives the parents a sense of pride and something to build on at home. It also allows parents to share pleasure with their children, one of the most productive ways of building up attachments and 'connections'. Above all, it is fun. As such a powerful tool, it is not surprising that music can be used very effectively to teach young children to learn, develop and behave appropriately.

The approach is based on *Music Makers* and you will find further information, suggestions for activities and a summary of the doctoral research evaluation in *Music Makers: music circle times to include everyone* by Mortimer (2005).

What you need

Start collecting or making musical instruments until you have a range of safe and attractive percussive and shaking instruments. You will also need some musical accompaniment. Perhaps you can harness some local musical talent and encourage a fellow professional or parent to play a guitar or keyboard. If not, a cassette recorder or CD-player works well. Make sure the quality of sound is good and have one adult on standby to manage the machine so that the music leader does not need to worry about it. We made our own CD with basic nursery rhymes and action songs and we all sang along to it. We did not simply let it run in the same old order, but used it to back up the songs we had planned for that session. Aim to keep the music as lively and individual as possible.

You will need a range of instruments that make a sound when shaken, when beaten or when scratched. Avoid blowing instruments which will need disinfecting each time they are used, unless the children bring their own. Make sure you have enough instruments for all the children and adults in the group. If you have a particularly popular instrument (usually the biggest drum) try to save up for more than one or help the children take turns fairly. We usually break 'band time' at least once to suggest to the children that they might like to choose a new instrument 'but only if you want to'.

Here is a suggested shopping list if you are buying a set of percussion instruments. How many you buy will depend on the size of the group, but try to get a good range. You can opt for colourful plastic instruments or you can buy 'real' instruments which can have a better sound though are not so easily sucked, dropped or banged. Look for a range reflecting different ethnicity and which are safe for young children.

Instrument	Have	To buy
Drums to beat with sticks		
Drums to beat with hands, e.g. bongos		
Tambourines		
Jingle bells in rings and jingle bells on sticks		
Triangles – attach the beaters permanently with string		
Castanets		
Cabassa		
Guiro		
Wood blocks and beaters		
Indian bells		
Maracas and a selection of rattles		

If you decide to make your instruments, make sure beans and pulses are securely contained. Remember that some uncooked beans are poisonous and be wary of younger children swallowing loose small parts or ingredients. You can make a range of sounds with dry pasta, rice, beans, sand, broken shell or gravel. You can make drums with saucepan lids or metal bowls with wooden spoons, and make use of large used coffee tins or upturned tubs which you can cover with bright paper or plastic.

The right space

You will also need a suitable area of your room to hold the music session in. Use a circle of chairs to signal to the families and children where to sit. The music leader should sit at the end of the circle nearest the wall so that the children are facing away from the rest of the play area. Keep the chairs close together to form a simple barrier; this way, the toddlers are less inclined to run around the room. Alternatively, you can have a circle of chairs for adults around the edge, and a 'song carpet' in the centre of the ring for the older children to sit on. Everyone in the room should join the music session (even the professionals who will be running the play session) – the only exceptions are babies asleep in buggies!

How to organise the music session

One of you should be the music leader – depending on who is confident enough to have a go. Use the session planning sheet below to help you plan the activities, aiming for 20 minutes' duration.

RUMPUS Music Time
Date: _____
Warm up
Hello song
Action rhymes/songs
Looking or listening games
Band time

Write in what you will do in each section and who will do it. This allows the whole session to flow smoothly.

Warm up

First choose a well-known favourite to signal the beginning of a session and become your 'theme tune'. *If you're happy and you know it* involves actions and familiar words, is easy to pick up and seems to be liked by most of the children. Another favourite could be *The wheels on the bus*. This should be your warm-up song at the beginning of *every* session. The warm-up song lets the children know that music is about to begin, makes them feel secure with its familiarity and immediately gives them an action to do in order to get going.

Hello song

You then need a greeting song to include and welcome all your families into music time. Make sure to include the names of any visiting siblings, toddlers or babies, even if they are sleeping. You should greet each child with a name, a look and a smile, perhaps a wave and a handshake or toe wiggle too. Ideally, you should encourage the children to look at you as you sing, and respond with a look, a smile or a wave. You should also encourage every single adult to join in the singing of this greeting song and you will find the older children join in too.

Never expect all the children or adults to join in singing all the songs. Both singing and doing actions at the same time are difficult for pre-school children, but are much more likely if the adults are doing it too. The author has no qualms in sharing her embarrassment with the parents and families with a laugh and a plead, urging them to join in too if they possibly can. Just a few never do (or at least it takes several weeks) – the trick is for the music leader to carry on regardless, to show good humour at all times and not to add to anyone else's embarrassment. Here is a simple version of a 'hello song', sung to the tune of *Tommy Thumb*.

Hello Daisy, Hello Daisy, (move in and establish eye contact)
Where are you?
Here I am, here I am! (wave)
How do you do! (take a hand or wiggle a toe)

Action rhymes/songs

Next move on to a few action songs or nursery rhymes. Keep the actions simple, starting with only one or two verses and building up until the children are familiar with the songs. Always try to have one well-known action rhyme and only introduce one new one per session. Encourage all the adults to model the actions and insist (with shared humour) that your fellow professionals do. Take the songs slowly to give everyone time to respond. Here are some ideas:

Old Macdonald had a farm.
Incy wincy spider climbed up the spout.
Two little birdies sitting on a wall.
Baa baa black sheep, have you any wool?
Twinkle twinkle little star.
Wind the bobbin up.
Miss Polly had a dolly who was sick, sick, sick.
Humpty Dumpty sat on a wall.

You might find the books *Okki-tokki-unga: Action Songs for Children* (A & C Black), *Music Makers* (QEd Publications) and *This Little Puffin* (Puffin Books) helpful resources to get you going.

Looking or listening games

If children are to learn to listen and respond to what they are told within their families, they will first need to develop their looking, listening and communication skills, and to develop a positive relationship with their parents or carers. Here are some simple ideas of games that will promote these to start you off:

- *Tambourine shake* – shake a tambourine and encourage everyone to shake all over until you bang it to stop. Share humour and praise the children by name for looking, listening and stopping.

- *Where's the sound?* – ask certain parents or colleagues to shake or bang an instrument behind their backs and encourage all the children to look in that direction. Then ask the parent to reveal the instrument and all cheer.

- *Pass the bells* – pass bells around the circle making a big noise (this is a lovely activity for getting parents to help their children), then repeat for a quiet noise. End with a big noise again and cheer.

- *Dinner on the train* – start with soft, slow voices and build up to loud, fast voices as you chant this rhyme. Add arm movements pretending to be a chugging train.

  Coffee (4 times)
  Cheese and biscuits (4 times)
  Chocolate pudding (4 times)
  Fish and chips (4 times)
  SOUUUUUUUP! (once with one hand held high as you 'blow the whistle')

Band time

Place your box of instruments in the centre of the circle. Invite children to come and choose an instrument and ask them to choose one for the grown-ups as well. Start the tape or CD. Encourage everyone to play when the music plays and stop when it stops. Later on, you can have fun playing loud and soft or fast and slow as well. Remember to praise children by name for looking, listening and stopping. Make sure that this is kept fun. Once the group has settled in, stand up and march round the room together (all of you) holding or shaking your instruments as you go. Children are fascinated by this and even the toddlers can join in independently and confidently. If at any point you feel that a child is opting out (for example, by beginning to have a tantrum or cling) say, 'It's OK to watch too.' After a few sessions, once it is all familiar, they usually join in.

Finish

Announce 'Play time!' Ask for the instruments to be put back into the box and get the toys out immediately (this helps with the 'transfer' from one activity to another). This is when those professionals playing with the children begin to distract them away from the circle to the other end of the room. Another professional takes orders for teas, coffees and refreshments for the families (asking parents what the children can have). Others help to close up the circle making a smaller circle for those adults involved in the behaviour session.

Close of RUMPUS session

After the behaviour and play session, come back together in the circle and finish with a 'goodbye' song, again naming each child and encouraging a look, a smile or a wave. You can invent your own or you can use this version, sung to the tune of 'Twinkle twinkle little star':

> Now it's time to say goodbye
> Matthew Bailey off you fly!

Tips for music leaders

The success of the music session depends less on whether you can sing and more on how well you can 'hold the floor with gusto'. Holding everyone's attention, keeping a balance and maintaining a flow are all important. Everyone would quickly lose interest if you sat and sang songs for a full half-hour. By varying the presentation from quick to slow, song to chant, quiet song to loud song, you can keep a flow going. You will find you can hold attention for ten minutes or so when you first get going, gradually building up to 20 minutes. Do not attempt longer at this age and stage. Use pauses to hold attention, stopping at key points of a song for others to join in (for example: 'One fell off, and then there were . . .').

Use your own movements (approaching the children close, or exaggerating the actions) to hold eyes and attention. Keep one or two surprises up your sleeve to renew interest, such as a puppet or props for songs like 'five little speckled frogs'. Use their names and your praise to hold attention. Keep children with a short attention span next to an adult who can help to focus their watching and demonstrate what to do to them directly. Try to keep this fun and non-confrontational. Make the children *want* to join in rather than tell them they ought to. If you really feel that you cannot sing (and this does improve with practice), then chant along to a musical tape and let others add the tunefulness. Children themselves do not sing in tune until they are about five, so you will not be on your own!

Chapter 5

Play time

In this chapter there are suggestions for crèche workers who will be entertaining the children.

The play session

There are three purposes of the play session. They are to:

- keep the children occupied while the parents or carers discuss their behaviour with other professionals;

- help children share, take turns, extend their play and concentration, and learn that playing can be enjoyable and fulfiling;

- provide ideas and models to the parents and carers of how to occupy and support their children using play and how to encourage their social behaviour. .

The emphasis should be on distracting the children and making them want to join in the play activities rather than forcing them to do so. At first, most of the children will keep moving between their carers and the toys as they seek reassurance. Once they are familiar with the sessions they will naturally tend to drift toward the other children and the play. Even babies and very young toddlers can be kept distracted and happy in this way, though they would be encouraged to go to Mum or Dad if they needed or wanted to. In this way, the play session differs from a typical crèche session.

Toy boxes need to be placed out as soon as the music session ends so that the children are distracted on to the next activity rather than left to complain about the end of the music session. Playing with young children is an active process and those of you with experience might need to suggest definite 'jobs to do' for any trainees or inexperienced staff who have not yet lost their own self-consciousness nor 'tuned in' to how young children play and interact.

The structured play activity might change from week to week. It is helpful if it can lead into a process or product that can be proudly shared with parents or carers at the end of the session. We usually have a 'celebration time' just before the goodbye song when we all admire and cheer what the children have been doing. Sometimes we use stickers or certificates to celebrate a kind action or good sharing. Even if the children are too young to appreciate these, it can make their adults proud and give them something to talk to each other about. Ideas for structured activities include:

- Making a collage/greetings card/hand painting/picture gallery.

- Playing with play dough.

- Mixing and baking activity.

- Matching game such as Picture Lotto, or simple turn-taking games.

- Model-making and craft activity.

- Giant floor jigsaw done in a group.

- A floor layout with construction toys and traffic game.

- Co-operative play with a train set.

There would always be free play choices on offer at the same time, with a genuine choice offered as to what the children wanted to play with.

Staffing levels

You will have planned the number of staff depending on the ages and stages of the children involved, recognising that babies will need one-to-one staffing though a group of older pre-school children could be happily and constructively involved in a structured activity such as hand painting or play dough for at least some of the time with limited supervision. The decision on staffing ratios is a pragmatic one rather than a legal one, since you are all in the room together and parents and carers are still present. The planning and review slots before and after each RUMPUS group allow you to review staffing requirements as you go along, depending on the needs and numbers.

Resolving disputes and celebrating progress

Use your own skills to resolve disputes as far as possible using positive approaches and distraction. Separate children into different activities if they are not getting on. Model how to ask for toys instead of snatching. Give clear rules and show the children what to do as well as telling them. *Expect* to have to repeat these over and over again with the same clear and positive tone of voice.

The ideal situation is that parents and carers can feel that *you* are well able to contain their child's behaviour and they do not need to be keeping a critical eye out and reprimanding their child regularly. When a parent feels 'watched', there is a feeling that they ought to be noticing and commenting on their child's negative behaviour continually in order to show others that they are in charge. Sadly, this does not work as a strategy for changing that behaviour. We are usually aiming in RUMPUS to move their management onto a more *positive* footing and this means that we frequently comment and draw parents' attention to the *positive* behaviours for a change. At the same time, we try to get the message across that we do know how difficult things can be at home as well, so that they feel believed and listened to.

Chapter 6

Changing behaviour

This chapter covers the behaviour management structure that lends itself to this kind of group, complete with diary sheet and celebration certificate.

Starting off

Once you have all finished the music session, interesting toys are lifted out to distract the children to the other end of the playroom, orders for refreshments are taken and the circle of chairs is closed so that the remaining adults can hear each other more clearly. The first five minutes or so when drinks are being organised allows time for the children to settle to play and for the parents and carers to clear their heads or chat to each other. Once drinks have arrived, there will be a combination of adults in your circle – the parents, carers and any young children or babies who are still on knees, the psychologist, and a ratio of one health visitor or other professional (see page 17) to each family group. The psychologist or an experienced health visitor usually takes the lead at this stage. Over the years, we have settled on the following format.

- **First ten minutes** a plenary session for everyone:
    - Introductions (where necessary).
    - Purpose of session (if unclear).
    - A round of 'good news' and 'bad news', e.g. 'one good/bad thing that happened to me this week was …'
    - General information on behavioural methods, e.g., on why positive behaviours work, or on using stickers and praise.
- **Next 30 minutes** or so work in pairs with a professional while the psychologist 'floats' between groups.
- **Last ten minutes** a plenary session:
    - Pulling it together.
    - Where next for each of us? 'One thing I hope to be able to do this week is …'

- Celebrations (the children gradually rejoin the adults as we celebrate their achievements this session).
- 'Goodbye' song.

We have found that groups take a while to 'get going' and seem to grow best when they start with families talking in pairs and then move on to discussion within the whole group. That way, acquaintances and confidences gradually strengthen and everyone gets to know each other. While we are in the kitchen preparing the drinks, we have a few minutes to talk about who will work with whom that week. Sometimes we opt for a professional who already knows the family well so that we can build on existing work. At other times, we feel that a change of face is needed in order to have the best chance of moving the family forward. Where possible, we encourage the same professional to work with the same two families each week so that a trusting relationship builds up.

The role of the professional

Often this professional will be a health visitor, family worker or Sure Start home visitor already familiar with supporting families with the behaviour of their young children. The professional will already have certain information about the family from the initial planning meeting (page 22) and from the questionnaire completed during the home visit (page 23). He or she begins by talking to one of the families with the other listening in.

Which behaviour did you really want to see changed?
How difficult are things at the moment?
What have you tried so far?
What seemed to work?
Can you think of a time when (child) behaved really well?
What was that about?

What do you think is causing the problem?
Who else is in your family?
What do they say about it?

As the conversation progresses, it will begin to feel more natural and the other family can be encouraged to chip in with similarities, ideas, coincidences or similar feelings.

The professional usually takes notes, asking the parents or carers first if this is OK with them. We use a notebook that the parents and carers keep themselves and bring back each session. Because these families have not usually been 'referred', as such, to a specialist agency, we feel that the notes are best kept open and owned by the families themselves. We can always borrow the book to write up case notes later if we need to.

The format we adopted was as follows.

Week one
Since the conversation has centred very much around the difficult behaviour, this leads naturally on to asking parents and carers to collect more information on their child's behaviour for us. We like to give parents and carers a definite 'job to do' after each session, which we write in the notebook. Asking them to keep a behaviour diary for a week is a good starting point. Usually we use the ABC diary format (see page 43).

Weeks two to six
By now the professional, family and psychologist will usually have begun to hatch a hypothesis about why the behaviour is happening and will have made suggestions for the family to try out. The best suggestions will have come from one family supporting another – these ideas are often listened to more than those that come from the professionals because they have been tried and tested! (However, we monitor them to make sure they are appropriate. For example, we have had some rather horrible suggestions

from parents on how to stop children from biting each other!) Suggestions are kept simple and practical, such as:

- Play for ten minutes each day at what your child wants to do.

- Visit the toy library with your child twice.

- Read a bedtime story together each night.

- Sit down together at mealtime and use a sticker for completing a small plateful.

- Return your child to bed each time he leaves his room.

- Get your child's eye contact and say her name before telling her what to do.

- Use a 'one-two-three' warning to show him you really mean it.

The suggestions are usually based on three kinds of approaches:

- A behavioural approach (this is explained more fully on page 42).

- Building positive relationships.

- Helping parents 'tune in' and interpret their children better (sometimes a small remark like 'Isn't she clever!' can lead to a completely new interpretation of why their child is being so challenging).

These last two approaches stem from Attachment Theory. You can read more about this in *Emotional Literacy and Mental Health in the Early Years* by Mortimer (2003).

The role of the psychologist

The idea that the psychologist (or other behaviour 'expert') should float between families arose for these reasons:

- Most of the families have already tried working with their own health visitor or home visitor and the RUMPUS has been suggested because 'more' is felt necessary. Therefore an added layer of new support and fresh advice is helpful to have.

- However, the psychologist's input ought to be shared around the families rather than limited to those deemed to have the more serious problems.

- 'Floating' allows the psychologist the time to move around the groups and spend time with each family and the professional they are talking with. The psychologist can then ask 'naïve' questions that help everyone tighten up their thinking. We believe this makes it more likely that the discussions and advice will be acted upon. The questions are usually asked of the professional with the parents or carers chipping in to make sure they are correct. The sort of questions that help include:

  - How have things gone this week?
  - What has already been tried?
  - What got in the way of the approach working?
  - Have you tried ...?
  - What would happen if ...?
  - When did (child) behave best this week?
  - What is the task you have set yourselves this week?
  - Is there anything you feel 'stuck' on?
  - What have you all decided to focus on next week?

A behavioural approach

This is a summary of the practical approach that we have use for changing behaviour, based on behavioural psychology and positive behaviour management.

Observation and assessment

The first step with a behaviour difficulty is to help parents and carers gather information. Not only does this provide the professionals with useful information, but it gives them 'thinking time' to work out what they can do about it, sharing any concerns or queries with the psychologist in the regular feedback and planning slots before and after each session. Sometimes the very act of parents standing back a little and observing what is going on gives them the emotional distance to think about the problem more objectively. Sometimes we see improvement straight away (though the problem behaviour might then 'shift' to something else).

Gathering information: week one
There are several methods which you can suggest to parents or carers for gathering information about a difficult behaviour.

An ABC diary
Ask parents to keep a diary in their notebook recording what the child was actually doing, what seemed to lead up to it and what the consequences were. Encourage them to write clearly and objectively, describing observable actions and using non-judgemental language. This is called an 'ABC' diary because it records:

A the **a**ntecedent – what led up to the behaviour or what was happening just before it.

B the **b**ehaviour itself in clear, unambiguous words. Encourage parents to use words like 'hit', 'threw', 'screamed' which help you actually visualise what was happening, rather than 'was aggressive', 'was disruptive' or 'was naughty' which are all rather vague terms.

C the **c**onsequences of the behaviour – what happened as a result.

Counting or measuring the behaviour
Sometimes a behaviour is so evident that you can actually count the number of times it happens during a session. Other behaviours can be measured in terms of their duration – perhaps a child screamed for ten minutes at bedtime or played happily for 20 minutes continuously after tea.

Behaviour charts
An 'ABC chart' can help to identify any factors that may be affecting the child's behaviour. Like the ABC diary, it allows you to gather information about all kinds of behaviour and not to identify the problem behaviour in advance. Ask parents or carers to record three or four significant incidents of 'difficult' behaviour on a chart such as this (which you can photocopy).

ABC Behaviour Chart

Remember, for every problem behaviour, collect information about an appropriate behaviour as well.

Time	What led up to it?	Behaviour	What happened next?

For every entry of a difficult behaviour, parents should be asked to record one occasion when the child was behaving appropriately or especially well. This provides you with information about the situations that work well for the child as well as those that are not so successful.

Problem solving: week two

- Once you have gathered as much information as you can about the child's behaviour, help the family select just one behaviour to work on first.

- Work with the family to decide on a hypothesis – what do we all think is keeping that behaviour going?

- Draw up a plan together to change the antecedents, the behaviour or the consequences (see below), writing suggestions in the notebook.

- Monitor progress over three weeks and then review your hypothesis and your interventions if you need to. Behavioural approaches take a little while to work because they often lead to a child testing the new boundaries for a while.

Planning changes: weeks two to six

What are the most common approaches you can advise families to follow for changing the *antecedents* to a difficult behaviour?

- Avoid likely situations by sidestepping them or planning around them.

- Distract the child and reduce the number of confrontations.

- Make sure the activity or the expectations suit the child's level.

- Encourage parents to use the child's name and gain full attention before giving directions.

- Ask them to give more positive attention before the trouble happens.

- Suggest that they give the child a warning of any changes of activity, like going out.

- Help them to anticipate problem times and be a step ahead.

- Encourage them to give clear directions and tell children what they should do as well as what they should not.

- Ask them to show the child what to do as well as saying it.

- Choose a few simple rules together and stick to them.

You can also help parents plan interventions that directly affect the child's *behaviour*.

- Stop the behaviour if they can safely and appropriately do so.

- Teach the child a new behaviour opposite to the first.

- Praise another behaviour incompatible with the first.

The third option is to plan interventions that change the *consequences* of a child's behaviour making it less likely to occur in the future.

- Help parents and carers to be absolutely consistent in managing the behaviour.

- Reward when the child is not doing the inappropriate behaviour.

- Ask them to ignore attention-seeking behaviour where it is safe to do so.

- Help them make it more fun for the child to behave appropriately.

- Star charts and stickers can also work well. Parents should never remove one once given. There is an example of a sticker chart on the next page which you can photocopy.

Hurray!

This week everyone was very proud of me because

I was given a sticker each time and here they are

Chapter 7

Evaluations

This chapter contains suggestions for evaluating this type of intervention and reporting back to management committees.

Evaluation and celebrations: session six

During the final session you need to try and make sure that each family feels confident enough to follow through the approaches without the support of the group, linking them up to health visitors or other professionals if necessary in order to keep them 'topped up'. Sometimes, you agree with the family a referral to another agency at this stage – hopefully that referral will now be seen as helpful rather than threatening. The session also provides an opportunity for collecting evaluations from all the families, either by talking with each individually, giving out a questionnaire or using the home visit after the group to gather this information. Here is a form that you can adapt or copy.

RUMPUS Evaluation

Confidential

Thank you for attending the group. We hope you found it helpful. Please give us some anonymous feedback to help us plan future groups – do feel free to be open with us.

Before the group began

Did you find the home visit helpful?　　　　　Yes　　　　　No

Why?

- -

Was the information given to you　Too much?　Just right?　Too little?

Did you feel prepared for the first session?	Yes	No

Coming to the group

Did your child enjoy coming?	Yes	No

Why?

What difference has the group made

to you?

to your child/ren?

What changes in the group do you feel are needed?

What activity did you find most useful? (Please number 1 as most useful and 5 as least)

> Music
> Talking in a group
> Talking one-to-one
> Play session
> Other – please tell us what

Was the venue suitable?	Yes	No

Would you recommend the group to other families?	Yes	No

Why?

Thank you for your time.
From the RUMPUS Team

Reporting to management

It is helpful if you can report back to management regularly on the perceived effectiveness of the RUMPUS groups. One reason for this is that it is an intensive intervention involving high staffing levels and unless you can show that the group actually changes referral patterns and patterns of parenting it might not be seen as value for money. We have therefore found it helpful to report not only on parents' evaluations, but our own evaluations of how we feel those families will now cope and whether we have been able to work preventatively. This sometimes involved using wider service statistics, including patterns of referral to CAMHS or to Social Services. Here are some examples of simple evaluation studies.

Evaluation studies so far

An early evaluation by Catterick Garrison health visitors (internal paper) found that the approach was value for money since it acted in preventing the need for further referral to the local CAMHS team. A diary study by the psychologist involved concluded that it had changed the whole pattern of referrals in this geographical area with fewer families needing specialist referral and, for those who need, better attendance at the child psychology clinic. The intervention has also been evaluated by Sally Robinson, doctoral clinical psychology student at Teesside University in 2003 (unpublished). Her study followed one RUMPUS group who met for one session per week over six weeks. The participants included six mothers and their children under five whose behavioural problems had been resistant to standard interventions by health visitors. Parenting stress of the carers was measured before and after the group, using the Parenting Stress Index – Short Form (Abidin, 1995). Two-thirds of the group showed an improvement in their clinical profile, with two of these having no remaining clinical problems. Parenting distress was lower after the group *as long as the parent or carer was able to attend regularly.*

The future

Our own plans for 'next steps' involve placing RUMPUS firmly within a whole scaffold of support for Sure Start families in such a way as these

50

groups arise naturally from other drop-in services. This way, we feel that they will be more parent-led and arise from clearly expressed family needs rather than what we decide is needed for them. We have seen enough benefits from the families and children involved to recommend the groups as a starting point for other areas faced with similar patterns of need.

References

Abidin, R. R. (1995) *Parenting Stress Index – Third Edition*. Oxford: The Psychological Corporation, Harcourt Education.

Bowlby, J. (1988) *A Secure Base: Clinical Implications of Attachment Theory*. London: Routledge.

Mortimer, H. (2003) *Emotional Literacy and Mental Health in the Early Years*. Lichfield: QEd Publications.

Mortimer, H. (2005) *Music Makers: music circle times to include everyone*. Lichfield: QEd Publications.

Useful books

DfES (2001) *Promoting Children's Mental Health within Early Years and School Settings*. Nottingham: DfES Publications (DfES ref. 0112/2001).

Green, C. (1997) *New Toddler Taming: A Parent's Guide to the First Four Years*. London: Vermilion.

Merrett, F. (1997) *Positive Parenting*. Lichfield: QEd Publications.

Mortimer, H. (2004) *Managing Children's Behaviour*. From the 'Early Years Training and Management Series'. Leamington Spa: Scholastic.

Mortimer, H. (2002) *Supporting Children with AD/HD and Attention Difficulties in the Early Years*. Lichfield: QEd Publications.

Mortimer, H. (2001) *Personal, Social and Emotional Development in the Early Years*. Lichfield: QEd Publications.

Quinn, M. and T. (1995) *From Pram to Primary: Parenting small children from birth to age six or seven.* Newry: Family Caring Trust.

Sutton, C. (1999) *Helping Families with Troubled Children: A Preventative Approach.* Chichester: Wiley.

Useful resources

Being Yourself hand puppets and therapeutic games for professionals working to improve mental well-being and emotional literacy in children. Send for a catalogue from Smallwood Publishing Ltd., The Old Bakery, Charlton House, Dour Street, Dover CT16 1ED.
Website: www.smallwood.co.uk

The *Understanding Childhood* leaflets available from The Child Psychotherapy Trust, Star House, 104–108 Grafton Road, London NW5 4BD.
Website: www.childpsychotherapytrust.org.uk

Videos, books and resources from Lucky Duck Publishing Ltd., c/o SAGE Publications Ltd., 1 Oliver's Yard, 55 City Road, London EC1Y 1SP.
Website: www.luckyduck.co.uk

Super Stickers (for reward and motivation) from P.O. Box 55, 4 Balloo Ave, Bangor, Co. Down BT19 7PJ.
Website: www.superstickers.com

The National Association of Toy and Leisure Libraries, 68 Churchway, London NW1 1LT
Tel: 020 7255 4600
Email: admin@playmatters.co.uk
Website: www.natll.org.uk

Useful organisations

Barnardo's, Tanners Lane, Barkingside, Ilford, Essex IG6 1QG
Tel: 020 8550 8822   Fax: 020 8551 6870
Website: www.barnardos.org.uk
Provides care and support for children in need and their families, with projects throughout the UK. A catalogue can be obtained from Barnardo's Child Care Publications, Barnardo's Trading Estate, Paycocke Road, Basildon, Essex SS14 3DR.

Cruse Bereavement Care, Cruse House, 126 Sheen Road, Richmond TW9 1UR
Tel: 0870 167 1677 (Helpline)   Fax: 020 8940 7638
Email: info@crusebereavementcare.org.uk
Website: www.crusebereavementcare.org.uk
Provides support and information for the widowed and their children.

Families Need Fathers, 134 Curtain Road, London EC2A 3AR
Tel: 020 7613 5060
Email: fnf@fnf.org.uk
Website: www.fnf.org.uk
A UK charity which provides information and support to parents, including unmarried parents, of either sex, and is chiefly concerned with the problems of maintaining a child's relationship with both parents during and after family breakdown.

Gingerbread, 7 Sovereign Court, Sovereign Close, London E1W 3HW
Tel: 0800 018 4318 (freephone advice line, 10am–4pm Monday–Friday)
Fax: 020 7488 9333
Email: office@gingerbread.org.uk
Website: www.gingerbread.org.uk
Supports lone parents and their children with financial, social and legal advice, and through social and practical activities. There are over 300 local self-help groups.

National Children's Bureau, 8 Wakley Street, London EC1V 7QE
Tel: 020 7843 6000 or 020 7843 6008 (library enquiry line: 10am–12 noon, and 2pm–4pm)
Fax: 020 7843 6007
Email: library@ncb.org.uk
Website: www.ncb.org.uk
A multidisciplinary organisation concerned with the promotion and identification of the interests of all children and young people. It is also involved in research, policy and practice development, and consultancy.

National NEWPIN, Sutherland House, 35 Sutherland Square, London SE17 3EE
Tel: 020 7703 6326
Fax: 020 7701 2660
Email: newpin@nationalnewpin.freeserve.co.uk
Website: www.newpin.org.uk
Offers parents and children an opportunity to achieve positive changes in their lives and relationships, and break the cycle of destructive family behaviour. There are several centres, mainly in the London area. Newpin offers parenting skills training programmes and includes a fathers' project.

Parent Network (Scotland), 15 Smith's Place, Edinburgh EH6 8NT
Tel: 0131 555 6780
Fax: 0131 555 6780
Email: info@parentnetwork.demon.co.uk
A programme of information, education and support run by trained parents for parents.

Parentline Plus, 529 Highgate Studios, 53–79 Highgate Road, London NW5 1TL
Tel: 020 7284 5500   Parentline: 0808 800 2222
Fax: 020 7584 55021
Email: headoffice@parentlineplus.org.uk
Website: www.parentlineplus.org.uk
Formed following the merger of Parentline and the National Stepfamily Association. Supports anyone parenting a child, including grandparents.

PIPPIN Parents in Partnership – Parent Infant Network, Derwood, Todds Green, Stevenage, Herts SG1 2JE
Tel: 01438 748487
Fax: 01438 748182
Website: www.pippin.org.uk
This national charity, which promotes positive early family and parent-infant relationships, aims to maintain and improve the emotional health of families during the period surrounding the birth of a new baby. It offers parentcraft classes, and a range of projects which include work with fathers.